Dear Parent:
Your child's love of reading starts here!

Every child learns to read in a different way and at his or her own speed. Some go back and forth between reading levels and read favorite books again and again. Others read through each level in order. You can help your young reader improve and become more confident by encouraging his or her own interests and abilities. From books your child reads with you to the first books he or she reads alone, there are I Can Read Books for every stage of reading:

SHARED READING
Basic language, word repetition, and whimsical illustrations, ideal for sharing with your emergent reader

BEGINNING READING
Short sentences, familiar words, and simple concepts for children eager to read on their own

READING WITH HELP
Engaging stories, longer sentences, and language play for developing readers

READING ALONE
Complex plots, challenging vocabulary, and high-interest topics for the independent reader

ADVANCED READING
Short paragraphs, chapters, and exciting themes for the perfect bridge to chapter books

I Can Read Books have introduced children to the joy of reading since 1957. Featuring award-winning authors and illustrators and a fabulous cast of beloved characters, I Can Read Books set the standard for beginning readers.

A lifetime of discovery begins with the magical words **"I Can Read!"**

Visit www.icanread.com for information
on enriching your child's reading experience.

For Ethan
—J.D.

To my wife Sasha, and my son Leon,
who give me the confidence to pursue my dreams
—C.K.

Author's Note:
Lincoln is known for his many memorable quotes. The ones in this book are taken from Lincoln's letters and other historical sources.

Bibliography:
Fleming, Candace. *The Lincolns: A Scrapbook Look at Abraham and Mary*. New York: Schwartz & Wade Books, 2008.
Freedman, Russell. *Lincoln: A Photobiography*. New York: Clarion Books, 1987.
Herbert, Janis. *Abraham Lincoln for Kids*. Chicago: Chicago Review Press, Inc., 2007.
Pascal, Janet B. *Who Was Abraham Lincoln?* New York: Grosset & Dunlap, 2008.
Thomson, Sarah L. *What Lincoln Said*. New York: HarperCollins Publishers, 2009.

Picture Credits
The following photographs are courtesy of the Library of Congress: page 28 (except the top photo of Lincoln), page 30 Lincoln without a beard, and Jefferson Davis; page 32 Wanted poster and Lincoln's hearse. Hearse photographer S. M. Fassett. Page 32 Mount Rushmore, South Dakota. Photographer Carol M. Highsmith.

The 1861 map on page 29 appeared in *Harper's Weekly*.

The following photographs are © Getty Images: page 28 Portrait of Abraham Lincoln (top), Photographer Matthew Brady; page 29 Presumed Slaves and Their Shack; page 30 Lincoln Visits Civil War Headquarters; page 32 Obama at the Lincoln Memorial. Photographer Alex Wong.

I Can Read Book® is a trademark of HarperCollins Publishers.

Library of Congress Control Number: 2016942119
ISBN 978-0-06-243256-8 (trade bdg.) — ISBN 978-0-06-243255-1 (pbk.)

Designed by Jeff Shake

17 18 19 20 21 SCP 10 9 8 7 6 5 4 3 2 1
❖
First Edition

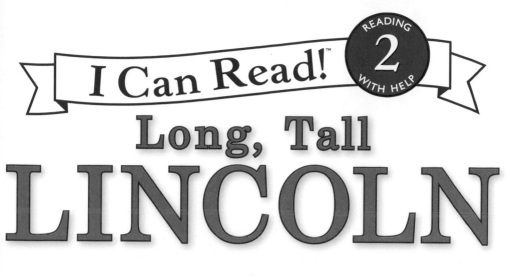

Long, Tall
LINCOLN

Written by Jennifer Dussling

Illustrated by Chin Ko

HARPER
An Imprint of HarperCollinsPublishers

Abraham Lincoln said it himself:

He was not a pretty man.

He was long and tall.

His ears stuck out.

His clothes were usually wrinkled,

and his pants were too short.

Lincoln didn't look

like a president.

He didn't always act

like a president, either.

But that didn't matter.

Lincoln acted the right way

for the country.

Most presidents were born rich.

Lincoln was born in a log cabin.

His family was poor,

and he didn't get to school often.

There weren't any schools nearby.

Instead, Lincoln chopped wood
and planted crops.
But he loved reading on his own.
"I'd rather read, tell stories,
crack jokes, talk, laugh—
anything but work," he said.

A speaker came to town
when Lincoln was a boy.
After the man's speech,
Lincoln hopped onto a stump
and pretended to be the speaker.

His friends laughed,
and Lincoln laughed, too.
But he also found out
he liked giving speeches!

When Lincoln grew up,

he had lots of jobs.

He worked on a boat.

He became a soldier.

He owned a store. . . .

It went broke.

He was very honest.

Once he walked miles to return

a few pennies to a shopper.

He had charged her too much!

Lincoln didn't seem like a man

who would be president one day.

But he studied hard

and became a lawyer.

He cared about people

and about justice.

Lawyers gave lots of speeches, too.

Lincoln liked that.

One night at a dance,

Lincoln met a lady named Mary Todd.

Mary was short and round.

Lincoln was tall and thin.

But they made a good match.

"His heart is as large
as his arms are long," she said.
Mary married Lincoln,
and they had four sons.

At that time, in the South,

the law let white people

own black people,

just as they owned a house or a horse.

Slaves were forced to work hard.

They were paid nothing

and were often hurt by their owners.

Northern states wanted

to get rid of slavery,

but Southern states wanted to keep it.

Lincoln did not like slavery.

"If slavery is not wrong,"

he wrote to a friend,

"nothing is wrong."

To change the law,

Lincoln had to join the government.

He won some elections.

He lost other elections.

But he kept going.

His speeches were very good.

People got to know him.

Finally, Lincoln ran for president.

He looked funny.

He talked like a country boy.

But people knew he was honest.

He won the election

and became the president

of the United States!

Before the election,

Grace, an eleven-year-old girl,

sent Lincoln a letter.

She had an idea—grow a beard!

She thought more people

would vote for him.

And she wrote,

"All the ladies like whiskers."

Lincoln took Grace's advice
and stopped shaving.
By the time he was sworn in,
he had a full black beard.

One month later,

America went to war,

Northern states against Southern.

It was a tough time to be president.

Even as president,

even during the Civil War,

Lincoln kept his humble ways.

Lincoln greeted White House guests
with "Howdy!"
He polished his own boots
and kept joke books in a desk drawer.
"If I did not laugh,
I should die," Lincoln said.

Lincoln was president,
but he didn't always act like one.
He wrestled with his sons
and let them keep lots of pets—
a pony, dogs, even a turkey.
Sometimes his kids broke
into important meetings.
Other presidents might have been mad.
Not Lincoln!

The war went on.

In 1863, Lincoln made a bold move.

He ordered that Southern states
free their slaves.

"If my name ever goes into history,"
Lincoln said, "it will be for this act."

The South ignored the order.

But up north,

black men joined the army.

They were ready to fight

for their country and freedom!

At last, after four long years,

the South gave up.

Slaves were free!

Lincoln did not hold a grudge.

The day after the war ended,

he asked a band to play "Dixie."

He knew the song meant

a lot to the South.

When Lincoln was elected,

many people weren't sure about him.

He looked funny and talked funny.

But people grew to love him.

Long, tall Lincoln became

one of America's favorite presidents.

How he looked didn't matter. . . .

How he acted did.

Timeline

1809
Lincoln is born.

1832
Lincoln buys a store—it fails.

1837
Lincoln becomes a lawyer.

1842
Lincoln and Mary Todd marry.

1846
Lincoln is elected to the House of Representatives.

1854
Lincoln is up for the Senate—he loses.

1858
Lincoln runs for the Senate—he loses again!

1860
Lincoln is elected president.

1861
The Civil War begins.

1863
Lincoln issues the Emancipation Proclamation.

1865
The Civil War ends. Lincoln is assassinated.

Slaves and their cabin

Was Lincoln always anti-slavery?

Lincoln thought slavery was wrong, but he also thought it would die out on its own. Then the Kansas-Nebraska Act of 1854 gave new states the choice to allow slavery. This, Lincoln could not stand.

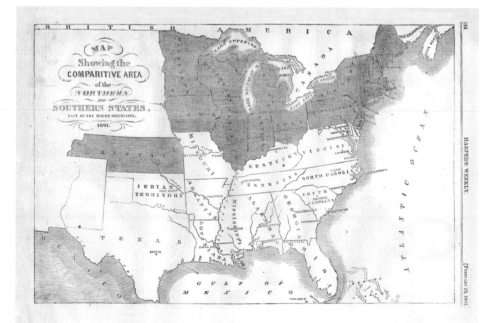

Map of the US, 1861

Did Lincoln care about the way he looked?

Not much. He once said, "If I had another face, do you think I would wear this one?"

Lincoln without a beard

What started the Civil War?

Following Lincoln's election, seven Southern states left the Union to form a new country—*with* slavery. They called it the Confederate States of America. Four other Southern states later joined. The Confederacy even had its own president. In April, the North went to war . . . initially to unite the country. Later Lincoln worked to free the slaves.

Confederate president, Jefferson Davis

President Lincoln meeting his generals

Department, Washington, April 20, 1865,

$100,000 REWARD!

THE MURDERER

of our late beloved President, Abraham Lincoln,

IS STILL AT LARGE.

$50,000 REWARD

Will be paid by this Department for his apprehension, in addition to any reward offered by Municipal Authorities or State Executives.

$25,000 REWARD

Will be paid for the apprehension of JOHN H. SURRATT, one of Booth's Accomplices.

$25,000 REWARD

Will be paid for the apprehension of David C. Harold, another of Booth's accomplices.

EDWIN M. STANTON, Secretary of War.

What happened after the Civil War ended?

Confederate General Robert E. Lee surrendered on April 9, 1865. Five days later, Lincoln and his wife went to see a play. A man named John Wilkes Booth sneaked into the president's box and shot him. Lincoln died the next day.

Wanted Poster for
John Wilkes Booth

Lincoln's hearse was drawn by six black horses.

How is Lincoln remembered today?

Lincoln and his looks are part of everyday life. His face is on the penny and the five-dollar bill. But his real legacy is freedom. He opened the way for men like Dr. Martin Luther King Jr. and President Obama to become leaders of the country.

President Obama
at the Lincoln Memorial

Mount Rushmore